MIX
Papier aus verantwortungsvollen Quellen
Paper from responsible sources
FSC® C105338

Dr. Tan Kwan Hong

Uncovering Key ASEAN Needs Vital to US Economic Legitimacy in ASEAN

Recommendations For Robust US-ASEAN Relations

Anchor Academic Publishing

Kwan Hong, Tan: Uncovering Key ASEAN Needs Vital to US Economic Legitimacy in ASEAN. Recommendations For Robust US-ASEAN Relations, Hamburg, Anchor Academic Publishing 2016

Buch-ISBN: 978-3-96067-064-3
PDF-eBook-ISBN: 978-3-96067-564-8
Druck/Herstellung: Anchor Academic Publishing, Hamburg, 2016
Covermotiv: © pixabay.de

Bibliografische Information der Deutschen Nationalbibliothek:
Die Deutsche Nationalbibliothek verzeichnet diese Publikation in der Deutschen Nationalbibliografie; detaillierte bibliografische Daten sind im Internet über http://dnb.d-nb.de abrufbar.

Bibliographical Information of the German National Library:
The German National Library lists this publication in the German National Bibliography. Detailed bibliographic data can be found at: http://dnb.d-nb.de

All rights reserved. This publication may not be reproduced, stored in a retrieval system or transmitted, in any form or by any means, electronic, mechanical, photocopying, recording or otherwise, without the prior permission of the publishers.

Das Werk einschließlich aller seiner Teile ist urheberrechtlich geschützt. Jede Verwertung außerhalb der Grenzen des Urheberrechtsgesetzes ist ohne Zustimmung des Verlages unzulässig und strafbar. Dies gilt insbesondere für Vervielfältigungen, Übersetzungen, Mikroverfilmungen und die Einspeicherung und Bearbeitung in elektronischen Systemen.

Die Wiedergabe von Gebrauchsnamen, Handelsnamen, Warenbezeichnungen usw. in diesem Werk berechtigt auch ohne besondere Kennzeichnung nicht zu der Annahme, dass solche Namen im Sinne der Warenzeichen- und Markenschutz-Gesetzgebung als frei zu betrachten wären und daher von jedermann benutzt werden dürften.

Die Informationen in diesem Werk wurden mit Sorgfalt erarbeitet. Dennoch können Fehler nicht vollständig ausgeschlossen werden und die Diplomica Verlag GmbH, die Autoren oder Übersetzer übernehmen keine juristische Verantwortung oder irgendeine Haftung für evtl. verbliebene fehlerhafte Angaben und deren Folgen.

Alle Rechte vorbehalten

© Anchor Academic Publishing, Imprint der Diplomica Verlag GmbH
Hermannstal 119k, 22119 Hamburg
http://www.diplomica-verlag.de, Hamburg 2016
Printed in Germany

Table of Contents

Chapter 1: Winning ASEAN's Hand in Marriage	5
Chapter 2: Crouching Tiger, Hidden Dragon (卧虎藏龍): The Untapped Potential of ASEAN as a Global Economic Force	8
Chapter 3: The Second Pivot: The Pivot from the TPP to the E3 Initiative	10
Chapter 4: Further Recommendations to a Constructive US-ASEAN Economic Alliance	13
Notes	19
Exhibits	22
About The Author	35

Chapter 1: Winning ASEAN's Hand in Marriage

With multiple choices of economic integrative mechanisms to choose from, ranging from the East Asia Free Trade Agreement (EAFT)[1] as proposed by China, to the Comprehensive Economic Partnership for East Asia (CEPEA)[2] as proposed by Japan, and not to forget the ASEAN Economic Community (AEC) that will foster intra-ASEAN trade and investment facilitation, ASEAN as an economic community has no lack of suitors and options.

Therefore, any US success for an effective and meaningful engagement with ASEAN as part of its pivot strategy hinges on its ability to uncover key strategic needs and elements of cooperation that other agreements or partnerships might not be able to provide. To be expounded upon in the second half of the article as key recommendations the Obama Administration might adopt, the acknowledgement of and assistance with ASEAN's developmental weaknesses are vital to longstanding US legitimacy and relevance within the ASEAN region.

In November 2012, during the fourth US-ASEAN Leaders' Meeting in Phnom Penh, President Barack Obama expressed a commitment to convert that forum into a summit. This will clearly enforce an annual participation by the US President in this newly created summit, raising the US-ASEAN relations to a "strategic level".

Additionally, as President Barack Obama transits into his second in office, the time could not be more ideal to pursue a US-ASEAN Expanded Economic Engagement (E3). This move would bode well to advance and institutionalize existing US-ASEAN engagements, and its material benefits are aplenty.

On the domestic front, it would compel U.S. departments and agencies that have been compartmentalized and uncoordinated to raise their levels of engagement, share information, and align government mandates with strategic objectives. If led by the White House, this new structure would incentivize key departments to participate in and plan for existing ASEAN-based frameworks, to engage the private sector with increased regularity, and to build political equity in the U.S. relationship with ASEAN. These are material gains that can only be accrued from the driving of interagency coordination and high-level alignment.

On the foreign policy front, the E3 will create a counterbalance to China's regional intentions. China, during the ASEAN Ministerial Meeting in July and the ASEAN Summit in November, clearly signaled an intention to weaken ASEAN in order to assert its claims in the South China Sea. By demonstrating increasingly aggressive behavior in recent months, it is questionable if the Chinese leaders will moderate their aggressiveness to a conducive level, especially in the near term. Therefore, by creating institutional frameworks that demonstrate a serious intent and long-term commitment to building ties with ASEAN, the E3 will serve as an effective signaling tool that convinces China on US's intentions of sustaining its high-level focus in the Asia Pacific region for the next decade, signaling an effective counterbalance to the Chinese regional intentions.

ASEAN will also stand to gain in many ways. Part of a strategy to strengthen ASEAN is to encourage investments in the region. By creating the E3, the US will encourage enhanced investments in the region's institutions. And with the support of the US, ASEAN's heightened statue in forums such as the annual East Asian Summit (EAS) will reap benefits, allowing it the confidence necessary to pursue vital regional and global interests in maritime security, nuclear nonproliferation, energy security, food security, and global health. The ultimate achievement of ASEAN interests can potentially lead to enhanced regional stability.

But the benefits to the marriage between the US and ASEAN with the E3 Initiative as the marriage proposal extend far beyond those listed above – Not only will it allow the US an opportunity in shaping rules, norms and terms of engagement with one of the fastest rising regional economy in the world, but it will also allow the US an alternative economic mechanism that can compliment the various weaknesses and arduous progress of the Trans-Pacific Partnership (TPP).

Chapter 2: Crouching Tiger, Hidden Dragon (卧虎藏龍): The Untapped Potential of ASEAN as a Global Economic Force

Long hidden behind the shadows of India and China, ASEAN's growing strategic relevance in the global economic arena can no longer be dismissed. The region boasts a combined GDP of $1.9 trillion, exceeding that of India; a population of 600 million people, which amounts to almost twice that of the US; and an average per-capita income mirroring China's.

The region will rank as the fifth largest in Purchasing Power Parity (PPP) terms (Exhibit 1), and is one of the fastest growing developing economic regions globally, with growth rates far outstripping that of the Middle East and Latin America (Exhibit 2). And if India is touted to be a global economic giant, ASEAN's GDP growth rate has already outperformed India's (Exhibit 3).

ASEAN would also be the region most dependent on trade, with a trade-to-GDP ratio exceeding 150 percent, outperforming that of many other regions. And despite the Asian Financial Crisis, middle-income countries like Indonesia, Malaysia, the Philippines, and Thailand have averaged a remarkable 7 percent annual growth rate since 2000. Also notwithstanding the 2008 global financial crisis, the entire sub-region bounced back brilliantly to soar beyond the 8 percent growth rate mark. This therefore highlighted a region that is resilient to global economic shocks, with the ability to adapt wisely through rapid policy adjustments.

Another avenue that might have piqued US interest on ASEAN lies in the region's strategic geographic location (Exhibit 4). The Malacca Straits is the world's second busiest shipping channel after the English Channel, and the second most popular oil tanker route, after the Straits of Hormuz. The Melacca Straits is the passage to more than half of the world's merchant fleet capacity annually, and disruptions in the straits would be catastrophic to global trade and US regional interest.

And with the materialization of the ASEAN Economic Community (AEC) in 2015, ASEAN will become one of the most integrated economic regions in the world.

The AEC constitutes an initiative to achieve the economic goals set under the umbrella of the ASEAN Community Blueprint (Exhibit 5). It aims to establish ASEAN as a single market and production base, a region fully integrated into the global economy that also achieves equitable economic development between member states, thereby turning it into a highly competitive economic region[3].

And apart from the economic benefits derived from engagements with a fast rising economic region, the E3 Initiative and other forms of ASEAN public or private sector engagements such as the US-ASEAN Business Forum[4] and the US-funded Maximizing Agricultural Revenue through Knowledge, Enterprise Development, and Trade (MARKET) Program[5] constitutes a hedging strategy towards the slow and arduous progress of the TPP.

Chapter 3: The Second Pivot: The Pivot from the TPP to the E3 Initiative

Despite the noble goals of the TPP in being a "high-level" agreement deliberately targeted at emerging trade issues of the 21st century[6], weaknesses that have yet to be overcome continue to plague the TPP.

First, the TPP is a rigid form of arrangement that requires members to eradicate almost all tariff and non-tariff barriers to trade. Few exemptions are granted, if any. Japan will have to liberalize its rice market. Countries with relatively closed economies will struggle to adapt. Countries with a protectionist posture on a few selected industries (e.g. due to union or domestic pressures or other reasons) might also be discouraged, even if they are willing to liberalize most other industries.

As such, this rigidity leads to the second problem – progress on concluding the TPP has been slow, arduous and fraught with difficulties. Despite being a concept mooted in 2005, eight years on, the TPP has been nowhere close to finalizing its membership base, let alone benefit from a liberalized trade between members. Although Japan, the world's third largest economy, has expressed interest to enter the negotiations[7], the TPP has became an issue of contention in the country's 2012 elections[8], whether it will ultimately enter the fray, remains at best a speculation. Not guaranteeing a major actor's entry will undermine the relevance of the TPP.

Third, the TPP might be seen as another US initiative to contain China, especially when the US currently remains as the leading entity directing the outcome of the TPP. Chinese hardliners might choose to perceive the TPP as an American-promoted, intrusively 'gold-standard' TPP that requires varying levels of domestic reform, so as to discourage China's participation in the program due to the differing nature of its economic architecture with that of China's state-controlled regime. This might undermine US-China relations as the TPP is being pushed through.

Fourth, given the rapid growth of the ASEAN economic force as mentioned above, no other equally-massive sub-region in the Asia-Pacific community can rival the collective growth of the ASEAN entity. The ability to ride on the ASEAN wave will be beneficial to the US. Unfortunately, by engaging in the TPP alone whereby only four ASEAN countries are involved (note that Indonesia, the largest ASEAN economy, isn't involved too), the US might be missing out on long-term growth.

Therefore, the pivot from the TPP to the E3 might prove beneficial as a hedging tool to the weaknesses of the TPP, and to better align the US to tap of the growth of ASEAN for long term gains. The author recommends that the US heighten the development of the E3 under the Obama Administration, while maintaining continued engagements with the TPP.

Maintaining continued engagements with the TPP is necessary for two reasons:

1. To send a signal of continued American interest in the region

2. And to prevent the TPP from plausibly falling apart or be reduced in membership to the four original signatories due to a leadership vacuum, for a diminished TPP might encourage alternative forms of multilateral trade agreements (such as the EATF and CEPEA) to take center stage among US major trade partners in the region, of which the interworking, norms and principles underlying such agreements might not be favorable towards the US.

However, the US might sensibly view the E3 as a more constructive vehicle in achieving American trade and economic objectives, at least in terms of implementation speed.

Also, as a backup plan in the event the TPP does not materialize full-scale in the short to mid term, the author recommends the pursuit of a comprehensive E3 with

ASEAN, supplemented with enhancing bilateral trade agreements with major partners such as Australia and New Zealand, as a viable and quicker alternative to extending the breath and depth of US trade engagements with the region.

Chapter 4: Further Recommendations to a Constructive US-ASEAN Economic Alliance

Despite ASEAN's growth, potential, and robustness as an economic region, ASEAN is still far from reaching its full economic potential. US legitimacy and relevance hinges on its ability and willingness to understand the fundamental economic needs and priorities of ASEAN.

The author proposes the I-4 Initiative: Infrastructure, Institutionalization, Incentivization, and Integration. Each recommendation/initiative are mutually supportive in formulating a vibrant US-ASEAN economic engagement.

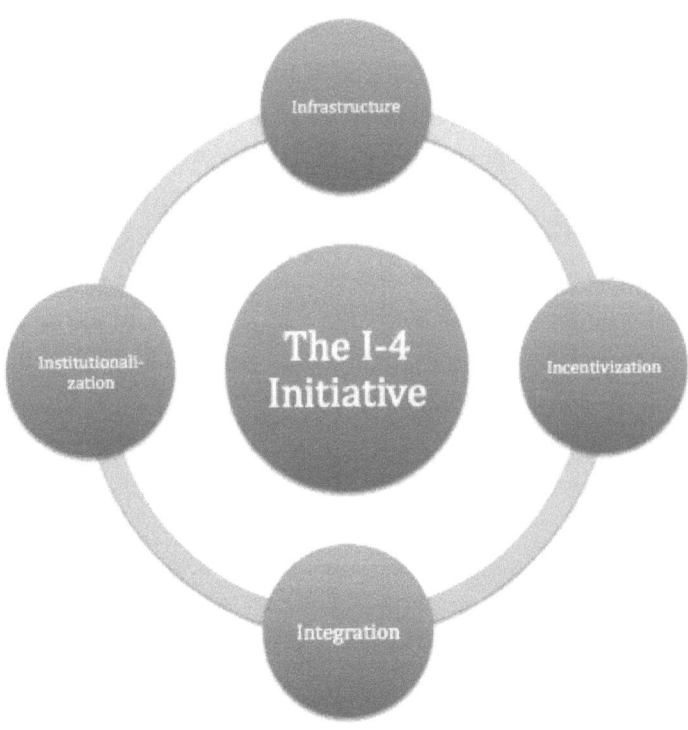

Infrastructure

Developing basic ASEAN infrastructure remains paramount to ASEAN's economic growth, and one of which is energy.

Despite the crucial importance energy in economic development, stunning insights emerge from current supply and demand balance in the ASEAN energy architecture. Electrification rates in ASEAN remained stunningly low. ASEAN, with a population of 567 million people, comprises of a startling proportion of 160.3 million people who do not have access to electricity, using twigs and leaves to cook their food.

Electrification rates vary widely throughout the ASEAN region, ranging from 10% in Myanmar to 100% in Singapore (Exhibit 6). With a projected GDP growth rate that is expected to supersede that of the world and of advanced economies till 2016 (Exhibit 7), the low electrification rates will further exacerbate the income disparity between rural and urban regions within a country. Income and development disparity might in turn have political and social implications within the country.

The region also faces a steep surge of demand for energy in the next two decades, so much so that despite having a considerable amount of coal and gas in the region, more will still need to be imported. The usage of oil and coal will remain as the dominant source of energy till 2030, and will continue to contribute to environmental damages.

Finally, enhancing energy efficiency is an often-overlooked factor in ASEAN energy policy developments. Several ASEAN countries face high transmission and distribution losses of electricity (Exhibit 8). This adds on to wasted resources, and to the cost of energy production.

Therefore, among all the infrastructural issues, energy is an often-forgotten issue that the US can get involved economically. The US can facilitate an energy-related business forum or economic society, whose members include energy and environmental companies from both ASEAN and the US. This will foster collaborations between ASEAN and US companies in energy projects that fulfill the large demand of energy in ASEAN. Projects on energy mass production, energy efficiency, energy trading and environmental conservation will generate jobs.

A research institute dedicated to research on US-ASEAN private and public sector energy cooperation, R&D development, and project implementation can be instituted. Government oversight and funding can be implemented concurrently on projects initiated through the forum, leading to public-private partnership (PPP) arrangements that will generate merit and public goods for the masses.

Institutionalization

Creating new and novel economic institutions will be crucial to jointly cater to the specific yet changing needs of ASEAN and the US. One emerging need is the rebalancing of efforts through the support of consumption and investment functions for an integrated ASEAN. Cross-border financial reforms are thus paramount.

The Obama Administration can therefore help to foster the institutionalization of key and novel market mechanisms and economic institutes that serves this function. For example, an ASEAN Economic Development Fund can be instituted with an initial injection of US funds, supplemented by fund contributions by ASEAN governments. Funds from ASEAN sources will then make up the largest proportion of funds in the long run. The benefits are multiple.

First, this initiative will allow governments of ASEAN states a readily accessible pool of funds vital for their economic and social developmental projects. Such a cross-border financial mechanism that improves the access of credit could help households and the government sector in reducing dependence on precautionary savings, in turn freeing up savings for investments.

Second, through a reduced dependence on precautionary savings, only then can the imbalance between ASEAN as a surplus entity and the US as a deficit entity be reduced. The savings rates of major ASEAN countries far exceed that of the US (Exhibit 9), and these savings can be better channeled to projects and investments that derive higher returns.

Third, with this cross-border financial institute acting as a substitute to US aid, the US might also benefit from the reduced reliance on any one ASEAN member on future US funds and aid. For example, US net bilateral aid flows to Myanmar alone amounted to about US$ 31 million in 2010 and to more than US$70 million in 2007 (Exhibit 10).

Finally, through the maturity of such a cross-border financial institute, further modes of fund raising, such as the issuance of bonds in the support of these institutes, can also be implemented. This will pave the way for a more mature equity and debt-trading market in which ASEAN currently lacks. The collective bond market size of major ASEAN countries are at present, paling in comparison with the bond market size of China and South Korea (Exhibit 11). The maturity of such financial markets will in turn pave the way for a joint ASEAN currency, if it ever desires so.

Incentivization

The US can also have a hand in incentivizing regional institutions and US businesses to invest in ASEAN. Grants or special economic arrangements can be granted to ASEAN-US business activities within specific sectors of focused, thereby encouraging US investments in ASEAN and even vice versa.

The goods and services export sector is a viable place to start. With most major ASEAN countries (except Singapore) facing a less-than-100 percent of total exports of goods and services as a percentage of GDP (Exhibit 12), such sectors are potential growth areas.

The time is also ripe for the US and foreign investors to participate in such opportunities. Via the ASEAN Economic Community (AEC) 2015, foreign investors will be able to enjoy up to a massive 70% of foreign ownership in ASEAN businesses.

Also, in order to incentivize ASEAN businesses to adopt US patents and trademarks, further grants can be given to ASEAN businesses to incentivize such a behavior. A lower cost of patent adoption will increase the utilization-rate of US patents, and reduce the need for patent theft, amounting to a benefit to all parties involved.

Finally, as ASEAN seeks to industrialize, technology exports and the exports of high end manufacturing tools and machinery from the US to ASEAN might also see a rise. Currently, Singapore is the biggest receiver of these exports, but such exports are vital to other developing ASEAN countries as they seek to industrialization and move up the value chain. Grants and special economic arrangements that incentivize ASEAN countries to enter into contracts for these highly valued products can therefore be viable. US total exports to ASEAN have seen an overall rising trend over from 2001 to 2011 (Exhibit 13).

Integration

To foster economic integration that will lead to the fulfillment of objectives as stated by the AEC, and for trade and investment facilitation between ASEAN and US, a range of principles and procedures will have to be aligned and integrated.

For example, investment policies, investor protection regimes, policies on non-discrimination, transparency and self-disclosure, market access rules and regulations all requires integration into a common set of rules and procedures unwaveringly abided by all.

Integrating each country's previous procedures into a simplified set of customs procedures, while simultaneously enhancing the transparency of the group's entire customs administrations, will bode well to enhance the overall economic integration with ASEAN and the US.

Also, an integrated set of principles governing the use of information and communication technology is vital. It will help assist policymakers and enforcement agencies on contemporary issues such as cross border information flow and local content requirements.

Finally, the US, in pursuing an integrated set of principles governing environmental protection, and on the safeguarding of small and medium enterprises (SMEs) – which generates the majority of all jobs in ASEAN and the US – can potentially utilize these avenues to extend its engagements to non-state actors, such as the various chamber of commerce, trade associations, non-governmental organizations (NGOs) and research institutes throughout ASEAN.

Notes

1. The East Asia Free Trade Agreement (EAFT) is a vehicle for economic integration favored by China, based on the ASEAN+3 membership base, namely, the 10 ASEAN member states, with China, Japan and South Korea. This effectively excludes the United States while inhibiting checks by non-ASEAN states on Chinese influence to Japan and South Korea.

2. The Comprehensive Economic Partnership for East Asia (CEPEA), also known as the Regional Comprehensive Economic Partnership (RCEP), is an extension of the 13-member East Asia Free Trade Agreement (EAFT) to include three more members, namely Australia, India and New Zealand. The economic rationale for including the six non-ASEAN states – China, Japan, South Korea, Australia, India and New Zealand – was that they have already concluded Free Trade Agreements (FTAs) with ASEAN, and that membership into the CEPEA was only sensible. However, five out of the six, all but China, are democratic economies oriented more or less towards Western economic principles and governance values. Therefore, this potentially China-balancing value of that distribution was not foregone on those who favored the CEPEA as a preferred alternative to the EAFT.

3. The AEC also promises an enhanced cross border mobility of goods, services, investments, and skilled labor. The reduction of cross border investment barriers will lead to the expedition of cross border investments within ASEAN and across ASEAN's economic allies, potentially leading to more mergers and acquisitions (M&As) in the future. Such is an avenue that the US can benefit from, on the conditions that it is being guided by enlightened foreign policies that focuses on developing an intimate economic coordination posture with its ASEAN allies.

Another aspect of the AEC lies in the free flow of services. Foreign ownership limit will be raised to 70% across ASEAN service sectors, along with other trade restrictions that will be reduced progressively. Liberalization of the 12 selected service sectors (Listed in alphabetical order: agriculture, air travel and transport, automotives, e-ASEAN, electronics, fisheries, healthcare, rubber-products, textiles and tourism) will occur progressively from 2012 to 2015.

Liberalization of foreign ownership limits and service sectors regulations constitute another avenue in which both the US can stand to benefit from with its close cooperation with ASEAN, though encouraging US businesses to acquire controlling stakes at fast growing ASEAN businesses.

4. US Secretary of State, Hilary Clinton, recently kick started the inaugural US-ASEAN Business Forum in July 2012, Seam Reap, Cambodia. This culminates in the meeting of government and private sector stakeholders from across the spectrum to come together and seek avenues to advance economic engagement and integration. Participating in this forum are multinational companies such as Boeing, Caterpillar, Chevron, DHL, Oracle, Peabody, P&G, ACE, Black & Veatch, Coca-Cola, GE, and Google, among others. It is hopeful that such a forum will stimulate job creation in various ASEAN countries, as well as allow these multinational organizations more ready access to ASEAN's natural resources and talent pool.

5. The US has been a supporter to the triennial conferences that encourages private sector engagement with the agenda of maintaining food security in ASEAN. For example, the US-funded Maximizing Agricultural Revenue through Knowledge, Enterprise Development, and Trade (MARKET) Program constitutes a critical avenue that encourages public-private partnerships (PPP) in the area of food security. The US also supported the Second Annual

Dialogue, a dialogue that brings together ASEAN Agriculture Ministers and business leaders in the food industry.

6. Retrieved from "The US and the TPP", USTR, 5 December 2012.

7. Retrieved from "Japanese PM Looks to Join TPP". The Globe and Mail. Retrieved 5 December 2012.

8. MAI IIDA (12 December 2012). "Major parties give themselves wiggle room on thorny TPP". The Japan Times. Retrieved 2012-12-15.

Exhibits

Exhibit 1: GDP in US Dollar Terms, adjusted for Purchasing Power Parity (PPP) Exchange Rates (2010 Figures)

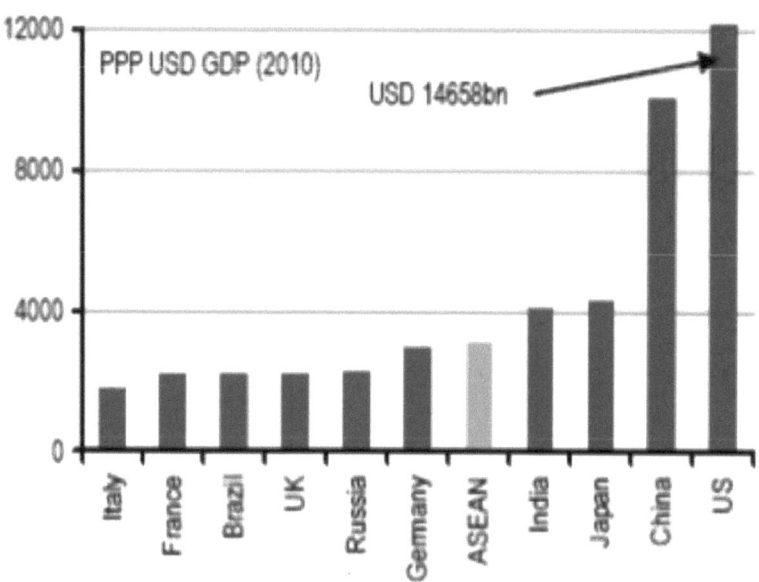

Source: UBS, UN, Haver

Explanation: When adjusted for relative prices to account for the relative differences in purchasing power, ASEAN will be propelled to become the 5th largest economy.

Exhibit 2: Southeast Asia's Growth has Outperformed Many Developing Regions

Trends in PPP Per Capital Income

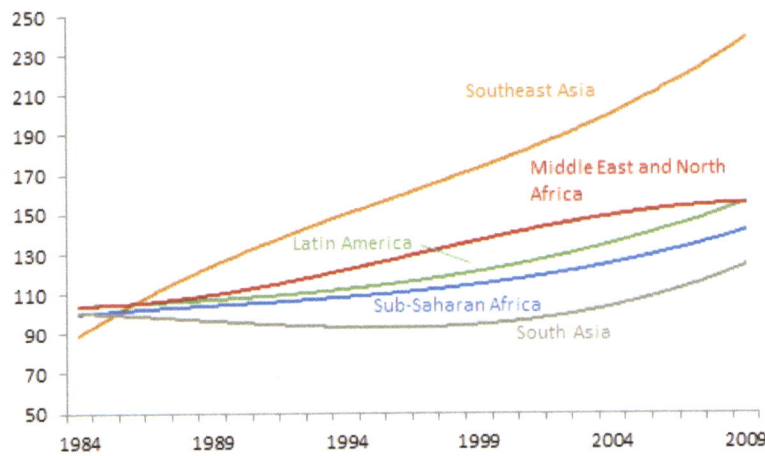

Note: Polynomial trend lines fitted to GDP per capita, constant US$ at 2005 PPP, 1984 = 100

Source: World Bank (excludes Myanmar for which data is unavailable)

**Exhibit 3: ASEAN's Growth Rate Outperformed that of India
(USD GDP Over Time)**

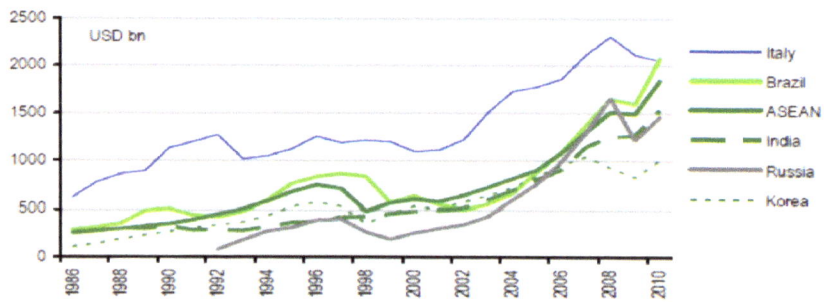

Source: UBS, UN, Haver

Explanation: ASEAN's growth rate in terms of GDP computed in US Dollar over time has already exceeded the growth rates of rapidly developing countries such as India and Russia.

Exhibit 4: Shipping Routes Around The Straits of Malacca

Source: Shipping routes from John H. Noer, "Chokepoints: Maritime Economic Concerns in Southeast Asia", National Defense University, Institute for National Strategic Studies, October 1996.

Exhibit 5: ASEAN Community 2015

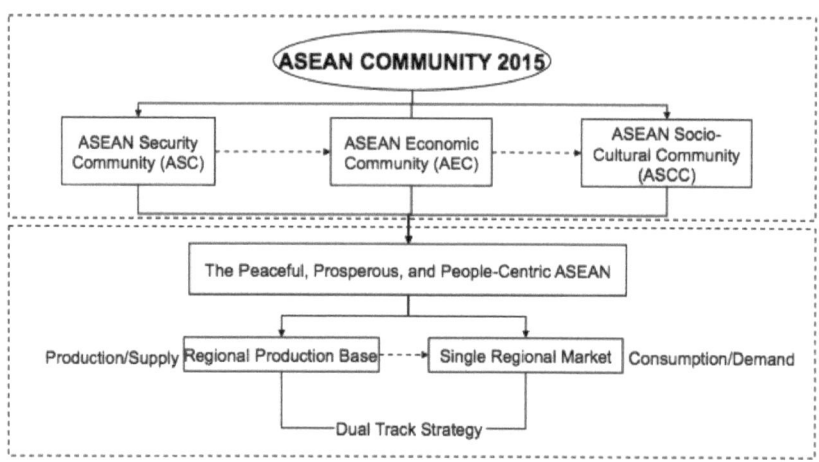

Exhibit 6: Electrification Rates of ASEAN Countries

Country	Electrification Rate (%)			Millions
	Total	Urban	Rural	Population without electricity
Brunei	99.7	100.0	98.6	0.0
Cambodia	24.0	66.0	12.5	11.2
Indonesia	64.5	94.0	32.0	81.1
Laos	55.0	84.0	42.0	2.7
Malaysia	99.4	100.0	98.0	0.2
Myanmar	13.0	19.0	10.0	42.8
Philippines	86.0	97.0	65.0	12.5
Singapore	100.0	100.0	100.0	0.0
Thailand	99.3	100.0	99.0	0.4
Vietnam	89.0	99.6	85.0	9.5
ASEAN Region	71.9	91.3	54.9	160.3

Source: International Energy Agency Electricity Access Database

Exhibit 7: ASEAN, World and Advanced Economies. Projected GDP Growth Rate till 2016

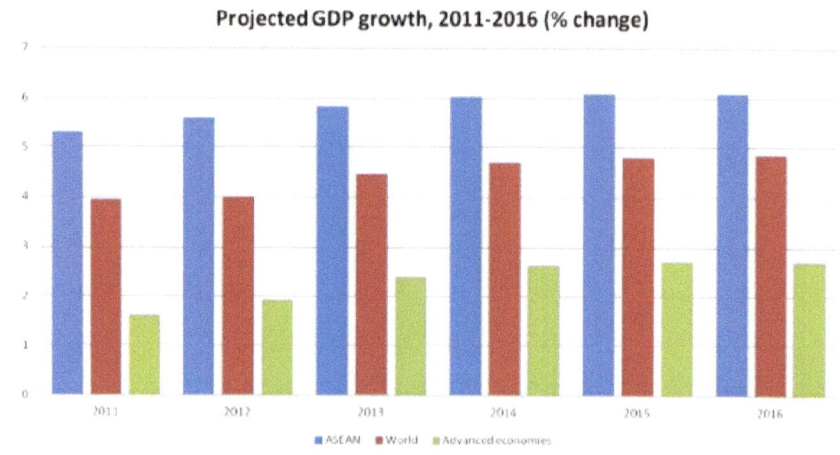

Source: International Monetary Fund, World Economic Outlook Database, September 2011

Exhibit 8: Poor Energy Efficiency in ASEAN

Country	(billion kWh)	Losses as % of total net generation
Brunei	0.218	6%
Burma (Myanmar)	0.22	34%
Cambodia	15.36	19%
Indonesia	0.26	10%
Laos	3.99	7%
Malaysia	1.91	4%
Philippines	7.5	13%
Singapore	2.16	5%
Thailand	8.78	6%
Vietnam	7.99	10%
China	181.15	5%
United States	260.58	7%
India	219.87	6%
OECD	662.78	7%

Source: Energy Studies Institute

Exhibit 9: ASEAN Countries Saves Far More than the US

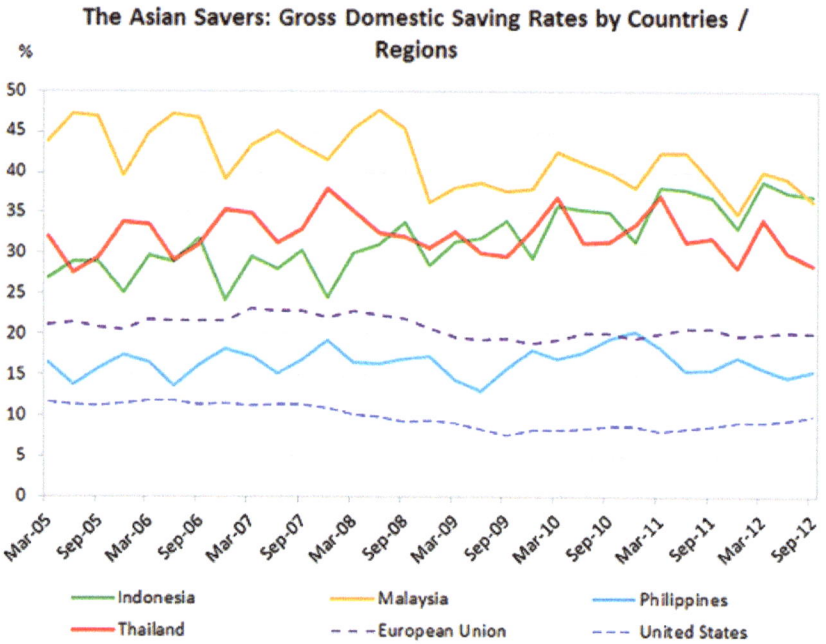

Source: CEIC

Exhibit 10: Net Bilateral Aid Flows from United States to Myanmar (US Dollar)

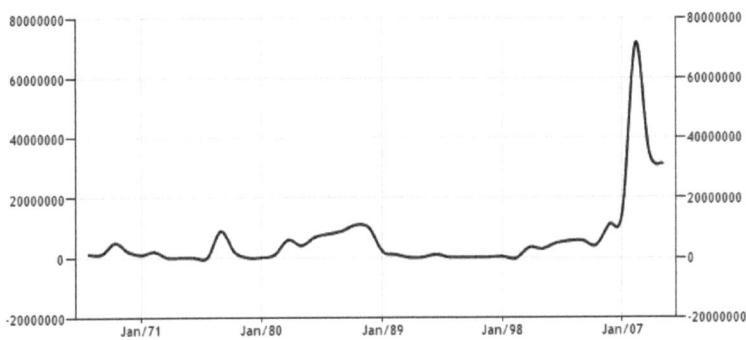

Source: Trading Economics

Exhibit 11: Breakdown of the Asian Bond Market by Country

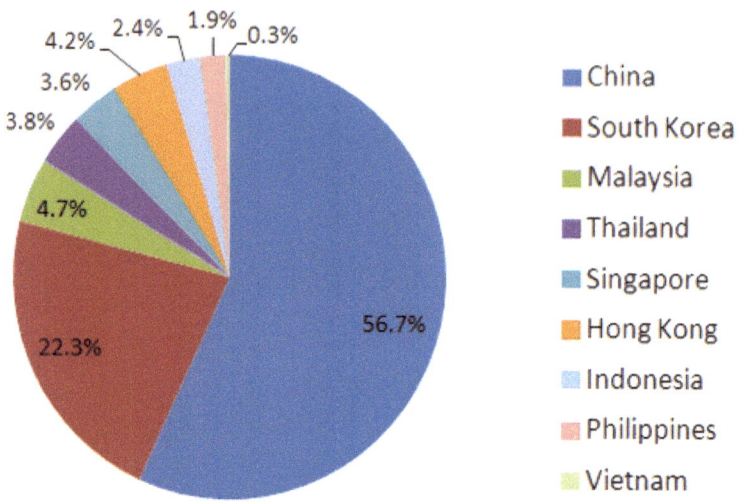

Source: Asian Development Bank (with data from various local sources)

Exhibit 12: Exports of Goods and Services as a Percentage of GDP

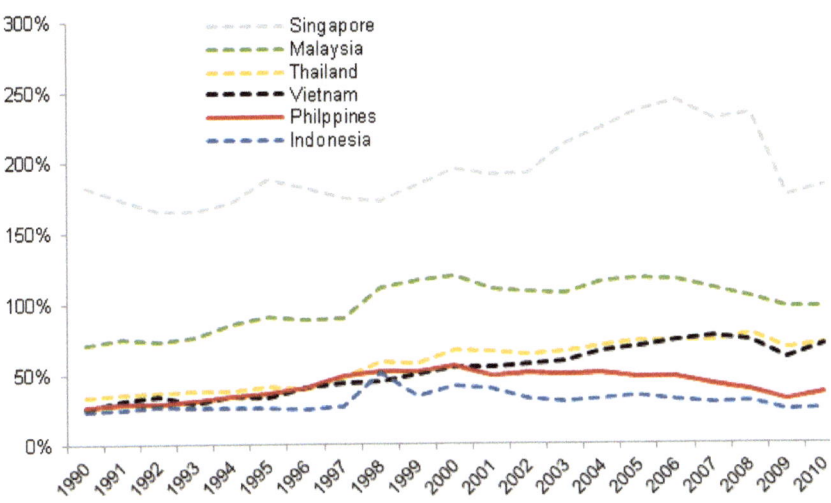

Source: UN Statistics Division (With Data from Respective National Statistical Agencies)

Exhibit 13: US Export of Goods to ASEAN, 2001 – 2011

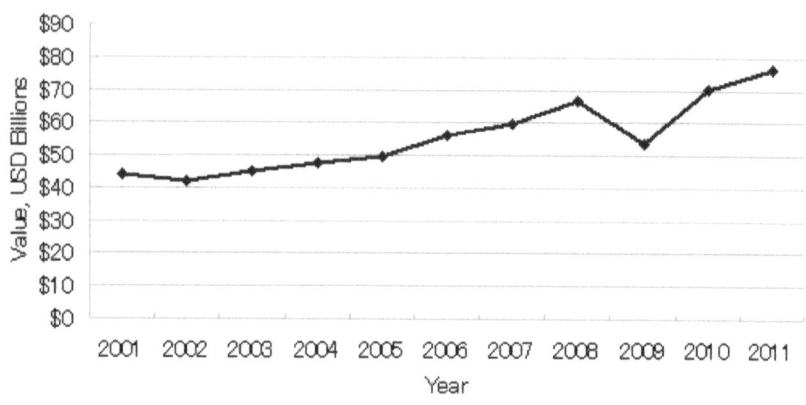

Source: United States Census Bureau - Foreign Trade

Explanation: The United States exported $76.24 billion in goods to ASEAN in 2011, an increase of 174.11% since 2001.

About The Author

Dr. Tan Kwan Hong serves as professor for finance, economics, business, leadership and human resource management. Beyond his involvement as a professor, lecturer and an academic writer, he is also an award-winning corporate trainer and lecturer and has given talks to more than 120,000 people on topics such as leadership, entrepreneurship, management skills, communication skills, persuasion, career management skills and personal peak performance.

Apart from accomplishing his Doctor of Philosophy, Dr. Tan Kwan Hong has 3 Masters degrees, in particular, the Master of Science (Finance) (With Distinction) from Grenoble Ecole de Management, the Master of Science (Human Resource) (With Distinction) from Edinburgh Napier University, and the Master of Education (With High Distinction) from Monash University.

He has also obtained 3 graduate diplomas to supplement his knowledge, in particular, the Specialist Diploma in Business Analytics (With Merit) from Temasek Polytechnic, the Post Graduate Diploma in Business Administration (With High Distinction) and the Graduate Diploma in Training and Development (With High Distinction), both from Aventis School of Management in Singapore. He has scored in the top grade category for all Masters and Graduate Diploma programs, and was the overall top student for several of these programs.

Dr. Tan Kwan Hong first graduated from the Singapore Management University with the Bachelor of Science (Economics) (With Distinction).

As an avid learner, Dr. Tan Kwan Hong has also obtained more than 150 different certifications in the areas of business analytics, finance, human resource, project management and sports science. He is a Certified Business Analytics Specialist (CBAS) and a Certified Associate in Project Management (CAPM). He is also a

Distinguished Toastmasters (DTM), the highest accolade achievable from Toastmasters International, only awarded to less than 1% of all members worldwide.

As a national science champion in his youth, Dr. Tan Kwan Hong was also the recipient of several scholarships, academic and university awards, national awards, public speaking awards, and also has a national-level strategy case competition championship title. He has also represented his country in regional conferences on academic and policy issues.

Dr. Tan Kwan Hong's corporate experience spans strategy consulting, financial research, education management and policy development. He can be contacted at www.tankwanhong.com and www.linkedin.com/in/tankwanhong.